GARDEN OF EMOTIONS
SCRIPTURE AND ART TO STRENGTHEN YOUR HEART
Copyright © 2018 by Dianne Iivari

Published by:
Healthy Life Press • Denver, CO 80219
www.healthylifepress.com

Author & Artist: Dianne Iivari
Designer: Judy Johnson

Printed in the United States of America

No part of this publication may be reproduced, stored in a retrieval system, or transmitted in any form or by any means—for example, electronic, photocopy, recording—without the prior written permission of the author.

Library of Congress Cataloging-in-Publication Data
Iivari, Dianne
Garden of Emotions: Scripture and Art to Strengthen Your Heart

ISBN 978-1-939267-31-3
1. RELIGION / Christian Life / Inspirational
2. RELIGION / Christian Life / Devotional

Bible quotations are from the Holy Bible, New Living Translation, copyright © 1996, 2004, 2007, 2013, 2015 by Tyndale House Foundation. Used by permission of Tyndale House Publishers Inc., Carol Stream, Illinois 60188. All rights reserved.

Most Healthy Life Press resources are available wherever books are sold. Distribution is primarily through *Amazon.com* and *healthylifepress.com*. Multiple copy discounts are available directly from Healthy Life Press. Wholesale distribution of this book is exclusively through *IngramSpark.com* and its affiliate, *SpringArbor.com*. Contact the publisher if you have questions about how to obtain a retailer's discount. Epublications of this book are available only through *Amazon.com* (KDP)—for all eBook readers—or by purchase at the publisher's website: *healthylifepress.com*.

Dedication

I would like to dedicate this book to God our Father and Creator who created me and gave me the talent to paint.

I would also like to dedicate this book to my best friend and ex-husband Keith who always believed in me and my artwork. He is now gone to be with the Lord, with the new heart he so desperately wanted.

I would also like to dedicate this book to my mom who believes in me a hundred percent and to my friendly Lumberjack Rob. I also dedicate it to all the artists who have not gone to school and have enormous talent, and to anyone who has overcome addictions in their life.

I would also like to express incredible gratitude to Judy Johnson for her amazing ability and insight to take my artwork and Scripture and highlight them with color and imagination.

I would also like to thank Dave Biebel. Without question he is my hero. God brought us both together and amazingly there was a connection in our family without even knowing it before we "met." Dave brings people's dreams to reality. He offered many words of wisdom and advice to help me through the process of publishing this book. I truly know that God brought us together for a reason. Without his dedication and sincere honesty and passion I truly believe this may never have happened.

Dianne Iivari

Awe

*Jesus responded, "Didn't I tell you
that you would see God's glory if you believe?"*
John 11:40

*The heavens proclaim the glory of God.
The skies display his craftsmanship.*
Psalm 19:1

Anger

So watch yourselves!
If another believer sins, rebuke that person;
then if there is repentance, forgive.
Luke 17:3

Sensible people control their temper;
they earn respect by overlooking wrongs.
Proverbs 19:11

A gentle answer deflects anger,
but harsh words make tempers flare.
Proverbs 15:1

Dreams

Hope deferred makes the heart sick, but a dream fulfilled is a tree of life.
Proverbs 13:12

Jesus looked at them intently and said, "Humanly speaking, it is impossible. But with God everything is possible."
Matthew 19:26

Commit your actions to the Lord, and your plans will succeed.
Proverbs 16:3

Now all glory to God, who is able, through his mighty power at work within us, to accomplish infinitely more than we might ask or think.
Ephesians 3:20

Despair

*In that day the deaf will hear words read from a book,
and the blind will see through the gloom and darkness.*
Isaiah 29:18

*Trust in the Lord with all your heart;
do not depend on your own understanding.*
Proverbs 3:5

*This is my command—be strong and courageous!
Do not be afraid or discouraged.
For the Lord your God is with you wherever you go.*
Joshua 1:9

Doubt

Then call on me when you are in trouble,
and I will rescue you, and you will give me glory."
Psalm 50:15

But Lord, be merciful to us, for we have waited for you.
Be our strong arm each day and our salvation in times of trouble.
Isaiah 33:2

Envy

Then I observed that most people are motivated to success because they envy their neighbors. But this, too, is meaningless—like chasing the wind.
Ecclesiastes 4:4

Don't envy sinners, but always continue to fear the Lord.
Proverbs 23:17

Faith

For I can do everything through Christ, who gives me strength.
Philippians 4:13

This Good News tells us how God makes us right in his sight.
This is accomplished from start to finish by faith. As the Scriptures say,
"It is through faith that a righteous person has life."
Romans 1:17

Faith shows the reality of what we hope for;
it is the evidence of things we cannot see.
Hebrews 11:1

Fear

You can go to bed without fear;
you will lie down and sleep soundly.
Proverbs 3:24

For God has not given us a spirit of fear and timidity,
but of power, love, and self-discipline.
2 Timothy 1:7

For I hold you by your right hand—I, the Lord your God.
And I say to you, "Don't be afraid. I am here to help you."
Isaiah 41:13

Hurt

A cheerful heart is good medicine,
but a broken spirit saps a person's strength.
Proverbs 17:22

It's not what goes into your mouth that defiles you;
you are defiled by the words that come out of your mouth.
Matthew 15:11

Even if my father and mother abandon me,
the Lord will hold me close.
Psalms 27:10

Hope

I say to myself, "The Lord is my inheritance;
therefore, I will hope in him!"
Lamentations 3:24

Yet I still dare to hope when I remember this:
The faithful love of the Lord never ends! His mercies never cease.
Lamentations 3:21-22

Then Jesus told him, "You believe because you have seen me.
Blessed are those who believe without seeing me."
John 20:29

Joy

You haven't done this before. Ask, using my name,
and you will receive, and you will have abundant joy.
John 16:24

You will live in joy and peace.
The mountains and hills will burst into song,
and the trees of the field will clap their hands!
Isaiah 55:12

Always be joyful.
1 Thessalonians 5:16

Loneliness

He will wipe every tear from their eyes, and there will be no more death or sorrow or crying or pain. All these things are gone forever.
Revelation 21:4

God blesses you who are hungry now, for you will be satisfied. God blesses you who weep now, for in due time you will laugh.
Luke 6:21

The Lord is close to the brokenhearted; he rescues those whose spirits are crushed.
Psalms 34:18

Love

This is my command: Love each other.
John 15:17

Anyone who loves a fellow believer is living in the light
and does not cause others to stumble.
1 John 2:10

Love never gives up, never loses faith,
is always hopeful, and endures through every circumstance.
Prophecy and speaking in unknown languages and
special knowledge will become useless.
But love will last forever!
1 Corinthians 13:7-8

Peace

I am leaving you with a gift—peace of mind and heart.
And the peace I give is a gift the world cannot give.
So don't be troubled or afraid.
John 14:27

The lowly will possess the land and will live in peace and prosperity.
Psalms 37:11

Work at living in peace with everyone, and work at living a holy life,
for those who are not holy will not see the Lord.
Hebrews 12:14

Sadness

Don't love money; be satisfied with what you have. For God has said,
"I will never fail you. I will never abandon you."
Hebrews 13:5

God blesses those who mourn, for they will be comforted.
Matthew 5:4

So you have sorrow now, but I will see you again;
then you will rejoice, and no one can rob you of that joy.
John 16:22

Security

Honor the Lord with your wealth and with the best part of everything you produce.
Then he will fill your barns with grain, and your vats will overflow with good wine.
Proverbs 3:9-10

God is our refuge and strength, always ready to help in times of trouble.
Psalms 46:1

Every word of God proves true.
He is a shield to all who come to him for protection.
Proverbs 30:5

Shame

Now you are free from your slavery to sin,
and you have become slaves to righteous living.
Romans 6:18

Sin is no longer your master, for you no longer live under the requirements of the law.
Instead, you live under the freedom of God's grace.
Romans 6:14

Keep watch and pray, so that you will not give in to temptation.
For the spirit is willing, but the body is weak.
Mark 14:38

Sorrow

God blesses those who mourn, for they will be comforted.
Matthew 5:4

God blesses you who are hungry now, for you will be satisfied.
God blesses you who weep now, for in due time you will laugh.
Luke 6:21

A glad heart makes a happy face;
a broken heart crushes the spirit.
Proverbs 15:13

Trust

He has given me a new song to sing, a hymn of praise to our God.
Many will see what he has done and be amazed.
They will put their trust in the Lord.
Psalms 40:3

Fearing people is a dangerous trap,
but trusting the Lord means safety.
Proverbs 29:25

Healthy Life Press • Denver, CO
Books, eBooks, DVDs

A Small, Independent Christian Publisher with a big mission—to help people live healthier lives physically, emotionally, spiritually, and relationally.

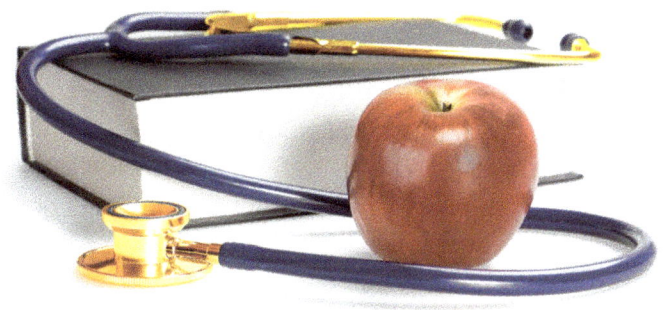

For a downloadable PDF catalog of our resources, and access to free sample excerpts from our books, visit: *www.healthylifepress.com*

1-877-331-2766　|　*info@healthylifepress.com*

www.ingramcontent.com/pod-product-compliance
Lightning Source LLC
Chambersburg PA
CBHW051249110526
44588CB00025B/2927